Other Books by Nancy Roberts:

Ghosts & Specters Of The Old South

Ghosts & Specters Of The Old South

TEN SUPERNATURAL STORIES

Nancy Roberts

Sandlapper Publishing Co, Inc., Orangeburg, South Carolina

GHOSTS AND SPECTERS OF THE OLD SOUTH

Copyright© 1974 by Nancy Roberts

First Published by Doubleday & Company
This Edition Published by Sandlapper Publishing Co., Inc.
Orangeburg, SC 29116

Photographs by Bruce Roberts

Library of Congress Cataloging in Publication Data

Roberts, Nancy, 1924–
  Ghosts and Specters of the Old South.

  Originally published: Ghosts and Specters / Bruce and Nancy Roberts; with photographs by Bruce Roberts. Garden City, N.Y.: Doubleday, 1974. With new introduction.
  Summary: A collection of stories describing ghostly apparitions and happenings in the Deep South.
  I. Ghost stories, American. 2. Tales—Southern States. [1. Ghosts—Fiction. 2. Folklore—United States.] I. Roberts, Bruce, 1930–   . Ghosts & specters. II. Title III. Title: Ghosts and specters of the Old South.

PZ8.1.R525Gh   1984   398.2'5'0975   84-14153
ISBN 0-87844-058-5 (pbk.)

MANUFACTURED IN THE UNITED STATES OF AMERICA

5 6 7 8 9 10   94 95 96 97 98 99

Contents

Introduction

WHETHER YOU BELIEVE IN GHOSTS or not—these stories are true. Or at least the people interviewed firmly believe they have seen ghosts. Certainly, the Governor's Mansion of Virginia is haunted. Several governors have seen and talked to the ghost. The dancing couple at Elmwood was seen by dozens of spectators.

For the skeptical, let me tell you that Joe Baldwin's light has been investigated, and even an entire company of troops from Fort Bragg were dispatched to capture the light. Railroad engineers so often mistook the ghost light at Maco Station for a signal to stop that the railroad was instructed to use two lanterns there instead of the usual one.

Introduction

The only license taken is to add a ghostly image to some of the photographs in order to reconstruct the scene photographically as it has been described. I hope the photographs of the haunted places give the feeling that "you are there."

Any Virginian will instantly recognize the Governor's Mansion at Richmond, and if you should visit the fort in St. Augustine, Florida, you will see that it looks just as it does in the pictures. If you would like to look for a ghost, the Reed Gold Mine near Charlotte is now a State and National Historic Site, marking the spot where the Carolina gold rush began, and the haunted gold mine is not far away!

This collection of ghost stories actually began twenty years ago with a series of Sunday feature stories on Carolina ghosts for the Charlotte (N.C.) *Observer.* A reporter on the *Observer* came back from an interview with Carl Sandburg, who said he had been reading the stories each Sunday and thought they would make an interesting book. These stories later appeared in book form in what was to be the first of three books of ghost stories.

The stories here have been done in the same manner as the stories for the first book: visiting each location, taking pictures of the actual site, and interviewing knowledgeable people. In general the journalistic approach is applied. In one case there is an actual photograph of a ghost light. The picture of Joe Baldwin's light coming down the railroad tracks was taken, believe it or not, on a dark and stormy night near Wilmington, North Carolina.

Introduction

With the hope you will enjoy meeting and knowing these real southern ghosts—

Sincerely,
Nancy Roberts
Charlotte, North Carolina

The Ghost of Captain Flint

THIS WOULD BE a spooky place after dark, thought ten-year-old Michael Shane as he looked at the large knife in the figure's hand. Of course, it was not a real man but the replica of a pirate with his cutlass raised ready to strike. Michael decided he would look around the museum at the old figureheads from ships, the name plates, anchors, and ship models. But all the time other thoughts were going through his head.

Was the ghost of Captain Flint sometimes heard and seen upstairs? Did the captain really die in a room somewhere in this building? Before he died did he give a treasure map to his pirate shipmate, Billy Bones? If only he had the chance to see for himself.

Michael listened to the museum attendant tell how this was once an inn for Savannah seamen. Pirates kidnaped unlucky men and boys who came here, took them out through an underground passage to the river, and made them serve on ships at sea. Then Michael had wandered away from the group and into another room. It was filled with boxes and barrels, cobwebs and dust, for it was a storage room and not part of the museum.

One corner was blocked off, which made Michael all the more curious about it. After he had pushed aside some of the barrels he found a heavy old table in his way and decided it would be easier to crawl under it. But all at once he caught himself. He had almost fallen into a large hole in the floor. It was really the mouth of a tunnel, long and shadowy.

He stretched one leg out behind him and found that the slope of the tunnel was gentle enough so that he could lower himself into it and still be able to climb back to the storage room. His feet found footholds between the squares of rock and he backed in still further. Finally his toes touched the flat floor of the passageway.

He was sure he had found the old tunnel to the river and if he walked far enough there would be the river and daylight at the other end. At the same moment he

Legend says Captain Flint died in this old Savannah building, now a popular restaurant.

heard a noise upstairs. A heavy door closed, not softly but with a careless crash. Michael's heart almost stopped. But he decided to go on for he thought he saw a tiny crack of light. He had almost reached it when he heard an outburst of wild and horrible laughter. And then the voice spoke.

"Batten down your hatches till you're spoke to, Billy. They are dogs and murderers, every last one of 'em. But you and I have a bargain."

For a while Michael did not dare to move. Then he crept quietly up to the top of the stairs. What was on the other side of the door? The crack of light was coming from beneath it. Did he dare to open it just a little? Now his hand rested on the knob. Suppose the door creaked? Ever so little at a time, he pulled the door toward him. He could hear the sound of curses and glasses clinking. There was a loud burst of song— "Fifteen men on a dead man's chest, yo-ho-ho and a bottle of rum. Drink and the devil had done for the rest," sang the voice loudly. Michael's face turned pale for he saw the man who was singing.

It was the one who was lying on the bed while another stood over him. Dressed like the pirates whose pictures he had seen, these must surely be the worst-looking men alive.

"By thunder, don't let 'em nail it, matey," gasped the man on the bed as he half rose and held out a large piece of wrinkled yellow paper to the other. Then he screamed "Brandy! Brandy!" his face twisting in pain as he sank back on the bed. His head fell over the side, mouth gaping, eyes staring fiercely without seeing. They closed and Michael knew he was dead.

The pirate with the scar on his terrible face came lunging toward him knife in hand and when the door swung open Michael stepped back in terror. The pirate brushed past him knocking him to the floor as he went by. Somewhere in the tunnel behind Michael there was a horrible scream and Michael's blood turned to ice. Then all was quiet.

Michael's courage slowly began to return and for the first time he could hardly wait to get out of the tunnel. Suppose everyone had left the museum. He was filled with fear. Would he ever see daylight again? What time was it? Where would his parents be? Michael wanted to run but the darkness was like a tomb where neither the living nor dead were able to see.

There was some light now streaming down from the room where he had entered the tunnel. All at once he noticed that the wall of the tunnel was slippery and wet, and he glanced at his hand as he wiped it on his shirt. It was red with blood!

At the same time Michael's foot struck something soft on the floor. Looking down, he saw the body of a pirate lying at his feet. Michael could tell that the man had been struck a sweeping blow with a cutlass and was very dead. Everything went black and he knew he must be fainting but it didn't matter.

When Michael opened his eyes again he was not sure

where he was. He knew he was stiff and sore and he wondered why—until he felt the hard, stone floor of the tunnel beneath him. Now all his fears returned. Reluctantly he looked around. But the body of the pirate was gone and the tunnel was empty except for himself.

He didn't wait long to see if anyone was coming, but leaping toward the sloping entrance, he clawed and scrambled upward to reach the room above. As he pulled himself along on his belly under the table and stood up among the boxes a frightening thought came to him. What if he was locked in this place of horror for the night—just him and Billy Bones and Captain Flint! He pushed boxes out of his path frantically. Some tumbled on top of him raising clouds of dust and he began to cough. His chest grew tight and his heart beat fast but he reached the door of the storage room and opened it. In the main room was a guide talking to a group of people.

"Now, some say Captain Flint, who was the most evil pirate of them all, died in this tavern. They think they hear an old sea song, something like 'Fifteen men on a dead man's chest, drink and the devil had done for the rest.'"

Hearing that, Michael began to run. He slipped passed the guide and was out the door. There in front of the

The pirate with the scar on his terrible face came lunging toward him.

museum was his parents' car and a policeman stood next to it talking to his dad.

"Good heavens, Michael. Where have you been for the last hour?" exclaimed his dad. His mother got out and began to hug him.

"Look at your shirt, Michael. You have some sort of reddish brown stain across the front of it. Did you hurt yourself?" Michael's mother lifted his shirt and looked at his chest and then at his arms. "Why, there isn't a mark on you and yet this looks like dried blood. Now, Michael we just can't take you anywhere again unless you stay with us. Someday you are going to get a bad scare if you keep wandering off like this."

And the Shanes drove off with Michael on the front seat. For years Mrs. Shane told about Michael's getting lost in the museum because she couldn't forget that she had never found anything to get those stupid stains out of Michael's good shirt.

. . . He saw the body of a pirate lying at his feet.

A house like Elmwood knows many secrets.

Dance of the Ghosts

BESIDE THE BLUE WATERS of the Rappahannock is a countryside that is rolling and peaceful. And among the woods and hills are huge houses that are just the place for ghosts.

A house like Elmwood knows many secrets for it has seen anger and love, laughter and weeping. Since 1774, generations of the Garnett family have played there as children, grown up there, and, one by one, their coffins have been placed in the center hall to be wept over by the rest of the family and then carried out the door to the family cemetery.

There is a real mystery at Elmwood.

Listen while the present owner of the house, Muscoe R. H. Garnett, tells you a strange story.

The days before the Civil War were full of gaiety at the great houses of Virginia and many parties were given by Mrs. Muscoe Garnett and her bachelor son, Muscoe Russell Hunter Garnett. Mrs. Garnett hoped that at one of these parties her son would meet his bride to be. She worried for fear she might die before seeing young Muscoe happily married.

In April of 1852 Mrs. Garnett gave one of her most beautiful parties inviting the neighboring families from miles around. She had no idea of what was to happen that night.

The party was in the ballroom and sounds of music could be heard in the front hall. Suddenly, the young lady playing the harpsichord stopped in the middle of the music and before her astonished eyes the keys continued to rise and fall. But the music had changed to the tune of a minuet.

At the same time guests who happened to be standing in the doorway of the room looked toward the hall stairs and gasped. For coming gracefully down the stairs through the hall and into the ballroom was a couple dancing the minuet. They were dressed in old-fashioned clothes and paid no heed to the guests who stepped back to make way for them. The man was handsome and the girl spirited and lovely.

They danced the length of the room and back into the center hall. Then before the amazed eyes of every-

The party was in the ballroom.

one, they seemed to float down the back steps and danced the minuet the length of the walk in the moonlight until they vanished into the darkness. The minuet stopped.

Young Muscoe Garnett was as surprised as his guests. He had watched the girl and found her very pretty. Now he dashed down the back steps and out into the garden. He was certain he would be able to find her in the bright moonlight. She must be somewhere behind the trees, among the large boxwood bushes, or perhaps she and her partner were lost and over near the cemetery.

He heard a rustling sound and he could see the old headstones. He was sure that someone was close by and for a moment he was afraid. But it was only a spring breeze blowing dead leaves about on top of the graves. The moon went under a cloud and the dappled gray headstones disappeared as darkness closed in around him.

Muscoe Garnett bumped into trees, he scratched himself on bushes as he tried to get out of the cemetery. Finally, his feet found the path and followed it. When he was sure he had almost reached the house, he bumped into something hard and cold. His fingers touched the surface and felt the outline of a lily carved in stone. He had lost his way and was back in the cemetery! His head swam and he thought he might faint, but the moon came out again and he was able to find his way back to the house.

Several times he dreamed of the girl dancing the minuet but he had almost forgotten her until the next summer when his mother gave another party. Once again the harpsichord, with no one touching it, began to play the delicate notes of a minuet. All eyes turned toward the center hall, for a couple was coming down the stairs and dancing into the ballroom. Each step was in perfect time to the music and the girl was the one young Muscoe Garnett had dreamed about. This time

They were dressed in old-fashioned clothes and paid no heed to the guests.

he decided he would close and lock the back door through which the couple had left before.

But to his surprise they danced right up to the door and did not stop to open it but simply went through it! There was no time to pursue them. By the time he recovered from his surprise and unlocked the door he knew it was too late, nor was there any moonlight. He went back to join his guests and sat down near a long mirror. Soon he began to notice a face in the mirror. It looked very much like the girl he had seen dancing the minuet.

He was afraid she would vanish before he could speak to her but she did not and he learned that she was visiting some friends of his and had come with them to the party. Many years ago her mother had visited here in Virginia and fallen in love with a young man but her father had taken her home to the North to marry another.

Within a few months young Muscoe Garnett and the girl were married. And over the years sometimes the ghostly couple still appears dancing the minuet down the stairs, across the ballroom, and out into the garden of Elmwood.

Instead of reaching the house he found himself back in the cemetery.

The Haunted Plantation House

THE HUNTER COULD SEE the tall columns of the house although it was growing dark. On each side of the road leading to it were huge oak trees draped with long gray moss that swung gently in the evening breeze. It was a gray February day and darkness had fallen before he realized he had lost his way.

But now he knew where he was. Many strange tales were told of this place and people spoke of sights no one could explain. He reined in his horse at the gate and sat

Darkness had fallen before he realized he had lost his way.

quietly for a moment looking toward the mansion. Was it really haunted?

Then he told himself, "I fear neither ghosts nor devils enough to take a long ride through the woods looking for a road in this darkness."

The horse hung back but with a sharp nudge from his spurs she lunged forward and galloped down the long avenue of trees up to the house.

His knock on the door was answered by the owner who was polite and welcoming. When the hunter told him he had lost his way, he invited him to have supper and spend the night.

"Tomorrow I will have someone lead you to the road to Savannah," promised his host.

As they talked, a breeze rose and the candles just inside the front door flickered. Shadows danced along the walls of the large center hall but the hunter was not afraid to have dinner and spend the night. The food was good and his host so friendly that he decided to tell him the stories he had heard about the house being haunted. The owner of the house smiled but did not look very happy.

"I would like to sleep in the haunted room, if you really have one," said the hunter.

There was a tiny flicker in the eyes of his host that might have been anger, but much to the hunter's relief he smiled.

"I am very sorry I have no haunted room for you but I do have the old library that my father used as a study and a bedroom. There are some curious books in it, with many stories about ghosts, although I really don't believe in them."

He opened the door to a large room with shelf after shelf of old books full of unusual pictures and fascinating information. The hunter was most interested in the family portraits that lined the walls of the room. He took the candle from beside his bed and walked over to each picture in turn, holding it so that he might look into the face.

There were eyes that were kind, eyes that were sad, eyes that were greedy, and eyes that were bad. Some of them made him uneasy as he looked into their depths and he wondered what sort of people they had been when they were alive. After admiring the portraits he climbed into the huge bed and was soon fast asleep.

He slept soundly until the grandfather clock in the room began to strike and on the stroke of three he suddenly awakened. The moon shone in faintly at the windows and made a path of silver on the polished floor. Although not directly in the moonlight everything in the room could be clearly seen. He did not know what could have awakened him for the clock striking had not bothered him earlier.

Then he heard a soft muffled sound as if someone was moving behind the curtains. Rising up quickly in his bed he saw that there was a man seated in a chair under one of the paintings. The man was in uniform and looked exactly like one of the portraits. He glanced at the picture above the figure. The frame was empty!

The hunter was now very frightened. What of the other portraits? His eyes were drawn to them and with awe he saw that all of the picture frames were empty. At the same time he began to see strange shapes moving about the room. When they became clearer he recognized an old lady in a black silk dress that rustled as she walked. In front of the mirror stood a young woman wearing a bridal veil upon her head. At the table in the center of the room sat a middle-aged man holding a piece of bread in his hand.

He could hear their voices talking, and a lady sitting on the foot of his bed spoke to another saying, "Are we to have no more music or dancing?"

"I think that depends on where we are going," said the other.

The military man in the chair seemed to be treated with respect by everyone but he was paying very little attention to them. His face was worried and sad. Soon he rose and began pacing to and fro. Once he walked so close to the bed that the hunter felt an icy breath of air fan his face.

The man in uniform suddenly turned and, walking over to the man seated at the table, tried to take the piece of bread from his hand.

"But what about my children?" the hunter could hear him say.

The moon shone in faintly at the windows.

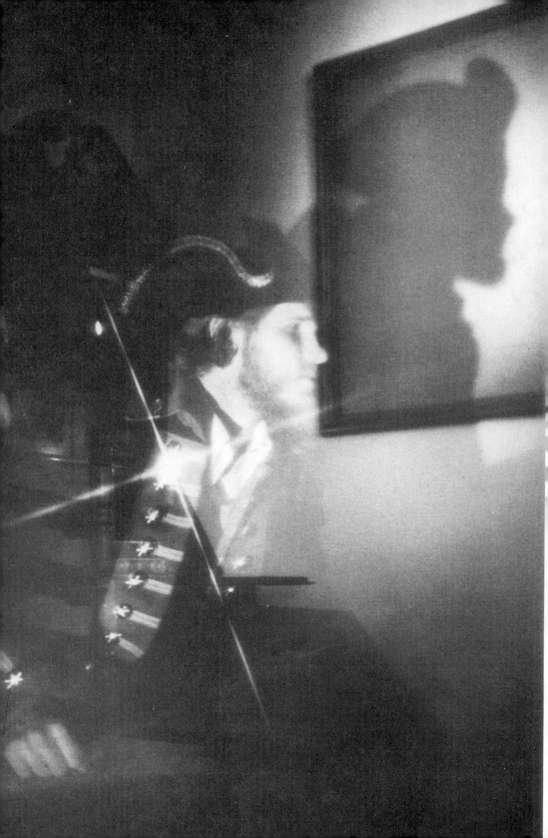

"I own this house and I have the papers to prove it," he said, beginning to wave his arms fiercely. But with an angry look the man at the table turned toward him and shook his head.

"Be fair! Be fair! Give up what is not your own," cried out the man in uniform.

"Don't let my family suffer, I beg you." The man at the table would not even answer him. The military man spun around with his face toward the hunter. It was dark with rage and his eyes glared straight at the frightened man in the bed. The sight was a fearful one and the hunter turned his head away. When he found that nothing happened to him and he felt brave enough to look around, he saw the figures in the room begin to fade. They seemed to melt into one another and soon all was dark, for the moon had gone down behind the trees. He fell into a deep sleep and did not awaken until late the following morning. His first act was to look around him at the portraits on the wall. There were the people he had seen the night before but they were all back in their frames.

At breakfast he asked his host, "Who is the man in uniform in the picture?"

"He was an officer in the war. This was once his house. When he died another man in the family claimed it and took it away from his wife and children. The papers she needed to prove she owned the house were lost."

The man in uniform suddenly turned.

"Were the papers ever found?"

"Yes, many years later some workmen were digging a well not far from the officer's bedroom window. They found a paper with writing on it that proved he was the real owner of this house. But by that time no one knew where the family had gone."

When he heard this the hunter was sure that what he had seen the night before was not a dream. The officer had really come out of the picture and was still looking for the papers to prove the house was his.

If you should ever visit Bonaventure at Savannah, Georgia, you will find that there is now a graveyard there. All traces of the house are gone but some who have been there late at night tell of seeing a man in uniform walking angrily about among the tombstones.

"Be fair! Be fair!" he cries out in the darkness. "Don't let my family suffer."

The Gray Man's Warning

MARY MACLENDON WAS NINE when she came to Pawley's Island, South Carolina, to visit her grandmother and the first thing the boy next door did was to tell her about the Gray Man.

"Lots of people around here have seen him," said Jimmy, "and this is the time of year he comes."

"Why does he come this time of year?"

"Because it's the hurricane season. He appears to warn people if there's a bad storm coming. Hasn't your grandmother told you? If you see him you'd better watch out."

"You mean something will really happen?"

He comes before all the bad storms.

"It sure will. You might get washed right off this little old island and your house, too, if you don't do what he says."

Mary shivered. "Have you ever seen him?"

"No. They say he comes before all the bad storms but I've never been out here before a hurricane. Ask your grandmother. She'll tell you about him. I've got to go now. See you later." And Jimmy Lattimore's tanned legs took off down the beach.

Mary walked along the water's edge until she came to the high sand dunes that protected her grandmother's house from the wind and the waves. After supper while her grandmother was straightening the kitchen, Mary said, "Grandmother, do you think I will see the Gray Man while I'm here?"

"The Gray Man! Whoever told you that story? I'll bet it was that Lattimore boy. Has he ever seen him?"

"No, but he says lots of people have. Have you, Grandmother?"

"My goodness, no. And I don't expect to!"

"Well, how did the story about him get started?"

"Years ago plantation owners had their summer homes here on the island. One of the girls was engaged to a young man who had been abroad for two years and she got word he would be home soon. She and her mother began to cook his favorite food and decorate the house. On the ride from his own house to hers, the young man and a friend who was riding along the beach with him began to race. He took a short cut through a swampy place and his horse fell. When he tried to get to his feet he found he was only sinking deeper into the mud. His friend tried to help him but it was too late.

"The girl was so sad she would walk for hours up and down the beach. Then late one afternoon she saw a man standing looking out over the water. He was dressed in gray and when she saw him clearly she was sure it was her fiancé. She ran over toward him but when she was just a few feet away, a cloud of mist swirled up from the sea around him and he disappeared.

"That night she dreamed she was in a tiny boat with big waves all around her. She could hear people screaming and see pieces of houses floating past. When she told her parents the next morning they decided to take her to a doctor in Charleston that very afternoon.

"A little while after they left the island a terrible hurricane hurled itself upon the coast. Houses were swept out to sea before anyone could escape and many people living along the water died in the storm. By now the girl and her parents knew that seeing the Gray Man and her dream that night had saved their lives. And that's how the story of the Gray Man started."

Mary stayed with her grandmother all summer. Day after day she jumped the waves liking the way it felt as the water sucked at the sand beneath her toes. She dug into the wet sand catching sand fleas and she collected shells.

A few days before she was to leave she went out on the raised walkway after supper. A man was walking along the beach. He was dressed in gray from head to toe. Mary started down the dune toward him and as she did he looked up at her. There was something about him that sent a chill down Mary's back but she made up her mind to see who he was. He walked along swinging his arms and she didn't know whether he had seen her. Perhaps she could catch up with him if she cut across one of the dunes.

When she reached the top, there he stood over near the water. But even as she stared at him he began to grow dim. Mary forgot to be afraid and began to race down the sand toward the water. It was too late for by now he was only a grayish blur and in a moment was gone. She was alone on the beach.

Mary was sure she had seen the Gray Man. And if the Gray Man appeared then a hurricane was on the way. She ran back to the house wondering whether her grandmother would believe her or not. While she was telling her about the gray figure on the beach Jimmy Lattimore's father came to their door.

"Mrs. MacLendon, we've just gotten word there's a bad storm off the coast headed this way. Can we take you and Mary into Georgetown to your house there?"

"You certainly can. We'll be packed in a few minutes," said her grandmother, and they were soon on their way. That night the wind and the rain battered

A cloudlike mist swirled up from the sea.

at their house in Georgetown and the rain was not over until early the next morning.

Mr. Lattimore came over to see if they would like to go out to the island with him. Everyone wanted to see what had happened. They heard many homes were full of water and sand and had been badly damaged by the storm.

When Mary and her grandmother reached their house they were very surprised. The doll's suitcase Mary had forgotten and left half open on the steps was still there. It hadn't been washed or blown away. There was no water or sand inside the house. And everything Mary had hung on the line across the porch the afternoon before was still there. Not even one towel had been blown away by the terrible winds of the hurricane!

Mary's grandmother looked at her and shook her head. She just couldn't believe everything was all right.

"You really must have seen the Gray Man, child. I've always heard that when he appears to someone, the storm never touches their home." Then Grandmother MacLendon had to sit down in the rocker and just rock and look out of the window for a while.

By now he was only a grayish blur.

The Little People

THE INDIANS KNEW the Pigeon River in Tennessee well. They also knew that the seldom-seen Little People lived in this forest beside the river and were nearby even when the Cherokees could not see them.

Little Doe often played in the forest or bathed in the sparkling waters of the river. Today she was alone but she was not afraid, for there was much to do. She strung leaves on a honeysuckle vine and tied it about her waist. She ran the vine through a large leaf from a tulip tree and placed it on top of her head. She found smooth rocks at the edge of the river bed which she was sure would be magic charms.

Today she strayed far from the path to pick plump, juicy wild blackberries. Late in the afternoon, as the sun slid lower in the sky, the forest was even more mysterious than usual in the dim light. Little Doe watched the waters of the river darken as the sunlight ceased to play on the silvery bubbles near the rocks and she thought of stories she had heard—stories of haunted whirlpools.

As the forest began to take on the look of night she remembered fireside tales of terrible slant-eyed giants and stone cannibals. Now, Little Doe began to be uneasy. She thought of her mother returning from the field with the rest of the squaws, of her father returning from the hunt. He would be sitting down to pull on the pipe she had watched him carve and she wished she were at home.

But where was the path that would lead her out of the woods? Little Doe had wandered far.

While her eyes searched the leafy green forest's gloomy depths for the path she had lost, something new joined the chorus of insects buzzing and small animals rustling in the underbrush. It was the very faint sound of drums. This frightened Little Doe even more for she knew it was not the time of the Green Corn Dance, the Eagle Dance, or any other celebrations in her tribe. It was not her people who were beating those drums. Perhaps they were war drums.

She realized that someone was standing not far away from her.

Was she in danger? Before she had time to decide, she realized that someone was standing not far away from her. Little Doe was terrified. She slowly turned her head expecting to see the stone cannibal or a slant-eyed giant. But it was neither. It was a very pretty little girl with long hair. Little Doe tried to speak but could not make a sound. She knew the little girl had not been there a moment before and could only be one of the Little People!

It was the Little People she had heard beating on their drums. She remembered what her mother once told her about them. They do not like for anyone to follow the sound of their drums. Did they think she had been trying to follow them? Would they be angry and perhaps try to kidnap or harm her?

The girl spoke to her and Little Doe was surprised that she spoke the language of her own people.

"Are you hungry? If you are, follow me," said the child. Somehow Little Doe could not have refused if she had wanted to, and she took the hand that was held out to her. There was a path just a few feet away that she had not even seen, and this was the path they followed. Ahead lay a dry stream bed full of rocks and, while Little Doe was thinking that the stones looked sharp and might hurt her feet, she was astonished to find that they had already crossed it and she could not recall her feet touching the ground.

Now they were approaching the darkest and most

dense part of the forest. The path grew narrow but still the briars and brush did not scratch her.

Her new friend would not let her even stop to rest and she was certain she was being led far from her own people and would probably never see them again. Although the forest had grown much darker, she noticed how shiny and bright was the hair of the other child. She would have liked to touch it, but did not.

Drums were beating all around her and it seemed that shadowy children were everywhere. She would have run if the hand had not held tightly to her own. They stopped at a tiny spring and taking a curved piece of bark the girl offered Little Doe, who was now terribly thirsty, a drink. She took it although it made her tremble for she feared it might be a deadly poison placed there by a magical power. But she felt much better after drinking it and now it seemed the girl who held her hand was pulling her along so fast that her feet had trouble keeping up.

The pounding beat of the drums faded and then were gone.

Suddenly she tripped and fell forward. When she looked up she saw she was at the edge of the forest and not far away was her own village. Little Doe pointed with her finger and glanced around at her new friend but there was no one there. She jumped up and ran toward the familiar figure of a woman. Even at this distance she knew it was her mother. As soon as she

reached her she threw herself into her mother's arms, pressing her face against her. Then she began to tell of her strange adventure.

Her mother looked at her feet and legs. There was not a scratch or mark on them from stones or briars. She was amazed. She caught Little Doe's hand in her own. It was clenched into a tight fist.

"What is in your hand?" asked her mother.

She opened it and there lay a tiny round object. They were not really sure what it could be but it looked like it might once have been a tiny drum.

"I think you have been with the Little People," said her mother. "Did you know they sometimes lead lost children home?"

Little Doe nodded, and she and her mother both stared in the direction of the forest. She thought of her friend somewhere out there in the darkness under the tall trees and wondered if she would ever see her again.

The girl who held her hand was pulling her along so fast that her feet had trouble keeping up.

Ghost of the Old Gold Mine

JEANIE HAD NEVER LOOKED for gold in her whole life but she decided she would after her grandfather told her the story of the old mine and the ghost there.

"How do you find gold, Granddad?" she asked.

"Well, you just take a pan, put some dirt in it from the stream, and swoosh it around until your gold settles to the bottom."

"Will you show me?"

Grandfather Bergen went out to the shed behind the house and brought back a rusty, round pan.

"All right. Let's go down to the stream in the pasture."

Nine-year-old Jeanie ran along the path ahead of him and Grandfather followed carrying a gold pan and a shovel. When he reached the stream he found a place where it curved around and there he dug a shovel full of reddish mud out of the water. He stooped down and, holding the pan just below the surface of the stream, began to shake it around and around.

Jeanie watched him take his hand and brush out some of the stones and gravel.

"Aren't you going to lose the gold, Grandfather?"

"Don't you worry. Gold's the heaviest thing there is. It will go right to the bottom of the pan and stay there." He pinched tiny balls of clay between his big fingers.

"Course we won't find anything much here. You have to go over to the stream near the old mine. Always heard that place was haunted and maybe it is. People used to come and pan in lots of streams around here during the Depression. That's when stories about a ghost at that mine out there in the woods got started."

"Who saw the ghost, Grandfather?"

"Well, it's been so long now, I don't rightly remember all about it. But this one miner was panning away thinking he was all alone when he looked upstream and there was another man panning too. The man had his back to him. He hollered at the fellow to ask how he

Stories got started about a ghost at that mine out there in the woods.

was doing but there wasn't any answer. That miner just kept right on and didn't even turn his head.

"The man thought he just hadn't heard him and since he was ready to head for home and going in that direction he waited until he was just a few feet away and spoke to him again.

"'You findin' any gold, friend?' The man panning still didn't answer and, looking at him close, he could see his clothes were graylike and so was his hat—kind of all one color. There was something mighty queer about it all and the miner felt the hairs on his arms stand straight up and he was cold even though it was hot.

"But he was bent and determined he would get that panner to say something, and he spoke once more.

"'Howdy, pardner,' he called out, and this time the figure turned his head. When he did it was the awfullest sight you ever saw. Underneath that hat there was just eyes, reddish fiery eyes that burned right through you, and where the face should have been there wasn't any face at all! Nothing but air and those mean, ugly-looking eyes hanging there staring at him.

"Well, the miner took off running through the bushes and trees, stumbling into one hole after another where folks had been digging gold. He was sure that thing was right behind him."

"You mean he was really scared, Grandfather?"

"He was just about as scared as a brave man can be."

"Did he ever go back?"

"He went back but he was mighty careful not to stay after sundown again."

"Look, Jeanie. There's color in the pan! See it? Right down in that black sand." Jeanie stared down at the gleaming, yellow flecks.

"Let me try it! I can do it." And she knelt down beside the stream with a pan full of mud from the bottom.

"You know the first gold rush in America started just a few miles from here," said Grandfather Bergen.

"A twelve-year-old boy found a seventeen-pound gold nugget in a stream. But that was just the start of it. Men came from everywhere. I hate to say it, but the ones that weren't bad when they got here turned that way later." He touched the tiny specks of gold in the bottom of Jeanie's pan.

"It's nothing but yellow metal. Why do men kill and cheat and steal over it?" said Grandfather Bergen to himself and he shook his head.

While she ate lunch Jeanie planned what to do. Every afternoon her grandfather took a nap and during that time she could easily walk to the old mine and back. As soon as she was sure he was asleep she started out toward the woods carrying the pan and shovel. She had no sooner reached the edge of the forest than she heard thunder and felt a drop of rain on her arm. But surely she would be better off in the woods than trying to run back across open fields to the house.

She scrambled through the underbrush, crawled under hanging vines and went around the placer pits. Breathless and exhausted she finally found the place she wanted to pan. It was on the bank of the stream just below the shafts of the old gold mine and if it was haunted Jeanie wasn't going to worry about it. Who believed in ghosts anyway! Gold was real—but ghosts? She had never seen a ghost in her whole life.

It took a long time to get a pan of dirt worked down to the gravel but Jeanie was patient. Her first pan did not have any gold flecks. She moved a few feet along the bank and found some tiny bits of gold in the next pan. But she still wasn't satisfied and she didn't notice how much darker the forest was growing as the storm came nearer.

About fifty feet away was a place where the water flowed over a little dam of sticks and stones that had caught on the rocks. In the pool of water below was a great place to pan. Jeanie had just dug a shovel of mud out of the pool when she saw someone panning downstream from her.

"Hi there!" she called out. There was no answer. What strange hands the man had—more like bony claws. He probably had not heard her because of the rumbles of thunder. She tried again.

"Hi. Are you finding any gold?"

This time the man turned his head toward her. Jeanie was terrified. There was no mouth, no nose, no face! Nothing but eyes that glowed like red-hot coals.

There was no mouth, no nose, no face!

She dropped her pan and shovel and ran. She ran through bushes and briars. She ran into placer pits where men had dug long, long ago. There was the sound of branches snapping and breaking behind her. She was sure the fiery eyes were not far behind her. A vine caught and held her ankle, and she knew if she could not free herself it would be too late. The burning eyes in the midst of the empty face would be staring into hers.

Tearing the vine loose she ran on until she reached the edge of the woods. Was something horrible running through the dark woods behind her? Jeanie raced across the field to the back door of the house. Her wet dress clung to her, her face was streaked by tears, and her legs and arms were a mass of scratches from the briars.

Grandfather was standing at the back door and he looked worried.

"Jeanie, I woke up when I heard the storm and I've been calling you ever since. Where have you been?"

Jeanie told him she had gone to the stream near the old mine to pan for gold. "And Grandfather, there really is a ghost that pans along that stream."

"I think there is too, Jeanie," replied her grandfather.

"You see, I'm the man who saw that ghost, and I never want to see it again. It's fun to pan for gold but there are lots of streams where we can pan. Another thing, I want you to promise me you will always go with someone else and not alone."

Jeanie was glad to promise.

Specter of the Spanish Castle

"Why can't we go somewhere that's fun? I don't want to see a stupid old fort," said Robert. "There won't be anything there!"

"Robert, don't you want to see the fort in St. Augustine that your great-grandfather once guarded?" said his dad.

"That was long ago."

"Did you know Castillo de San Marcos is haunted?"

"Haunted by what?"

"By the ghosts of the men who were once there."

"Oh, Dad, you don't believe in ghosts."

"Sometimes I think I do."

By now they had reached the fort. What if he should

see a ghost, maybe even the ghost of his great-grandfather. Robert saw the high, thick walls of the old fort rising before him. Over the Spanish fort now flew the American flag. It really did look like a haunted castle. He knew he had to explore it and find out for himself.

Robert thought about the picture of his great-grandfather on the wall at home. The handsome, bearded face in the United States officer's uniform and hat. He must have crossed this same drawbridge, gazed across the water in the moat. Would he meet him here, somewhere inside these monstrous stone walls? He was so eager to see everything that he soon left his parents behind.

"Robert, Robert!" called his father. "How many times must I tell you not to get ahead of us. Your mother and I want to read the history of the fort as we go along." But Robert soon began to get ahead of them. Again his father called to him. "Robert, if you are not going to stay with us, it would be much better for you to go wherever you want to and meet us back at the drawbridge in an hour. It's three o'clock. Why don't you meet us there at four?

"Be sure to check your watch and be there on time," warned his father.

"I will. I will," promised Robert. It was much more fun to go alone. He never thought about the old fort being scary, for he was pretending to be a soldier like

By now they had reached the fort.

his great-grandfather. People in olden days had all the
luck—Indians to fight, outlaws to capture. Why
couldn't he have lived then?

Imagining that he was a Spanish soldier of long ago,
he looked out over the Matanzas River toward the
ocean, pretending enemy ships were on the way. Then
he noticed something was bobbing in the moat far below
him. Perhaps it was the head of an Indian escaping from
the fort. But the Seminole Indians were kept safely in
the dungeons below during the war, were they not?
He decided to go down and see where the prisoners
were held.

The cells were dark, gloomy, and quiet as a graveyard. His skin crawled when he thought of staying in
here, perhaps with rats and scorpions! The walls and
floors were damp to the touch. High above him was a
tiny window. There was a sharp crash of thunder and
the cell began to grow dark. Robert was afraid for the
first time. He looked out the door of the cell and saw
large drops of rain spattering the dust. He knew that
he ought to hurry to meet his parents.

It was now so dark he could hardly see. Flash after
flash of lightning lighted the walls of the small room.
He wanted to get out. He thought about the prisoners.
Was this how they had felt in this same tiny room? He
wanted to scream, but who would hear him above the
noise of the storm?

Gradually his eyes became used to the dim light and
as they did he could not believe what he saw!

There were two other people in the room with him. One was an Indian with the most proud and handsome face he had ever seen. The other was an officer in the U. S. Army. The two men were talking and they were so close that if he had wanted to—which he did not!— he could have reached out his hand and touched them.

Instead he shrunk back against the wall greatly afraid they might see him. But soon he realized they did not know he was in the room. The officer shook his head gravely.

"Wildcat, I know what they will do to you if you remain here for you are the son of a king. But I cannot help you." The Indian held out both hands, palms upward, toward the other man and the boy knew he was asking for something. He watched the face of the officer. It was so familiar he thought he had seen it in a dream. But then he remembered the face in the picture at home and it was the same. This man he was watching was his own great-grandfather! His legs began to give way beneath him and for a moment he was sure he was drifting off as he did in his bed when he was falling asleep.

Was this a dream? A loud clap of thunder brought him back and there were the two men standing just as before. But now he saw kindness, even sympathy on the face of the officer wearing the gold braid. As he watched, the soldier deliberately turned his back to the room and stood staring out the door.

The Indian ran toward the wall of the cell and, using

something in his hand, began to saw through one of the bars on the tiny window. Robert thought he ought to warn the officer that the prisoner was about to escape. He shouted at him but he did not turn around. The Indian drew himself up like a cat, eased the length of his body through the small opening, and was gone. The man in the doorway was gone too.

Badly frightened, Robert was about to dash out despite the rain when he saw a group of officers walking across the yard straight toward the door of his cell as if they didn't even notice the heavy rain. They came in and immediately began to shout angrily.

"The son of the Indian king is gone. Wildcat has escaped!" Off they ran scattering in every direction.

Robert ran also. He ran through the downpour of rain. He ran until his chest hurt but he didn't care. When he reached the drawbridge he found his parents just inside the fort waiting for him.

"Tell me who Wildcat was," he asked grasping his father's arm.

"What is the matter with you, Robert? Why are you so excited?"

"Just tell me who he was, please, Dad."

"Wildcat was once imprisoned here and escaped. He was the son of Philip, an Indian king."

One was an Indian with the most proud and handsome face he had ever seen.

"When did he escape?"

"I think it was sometime during your great-grand-father's time. Why?"

Robert did not answer. He was thinking about all that had happened.

Ghost of the Governor's Mansion

THE GOVERNOR OF VIRGINIA lives in a haunted mansion where strange things happen. The present governor of Virginia, Governor Linwood Holton, thinks a ghost may haunt this old house in Richmond.

The ghost was first seen in the early 1890s. Governor Philip McKinney sat in a chair before the fire writing a letter. All the children were asleep and the house was so quiet he could hear the clock on the mantel tick-tick-tocking away.

As he wrote he began to notice a very slight sound as if a woman's heels were lightly tapping down the floor of the hall behind him. He rose from his chair thinking it was his wife but when he looked down the long hall it was empty.

I must have imagined it, thought the governor. I am more tired than I realized. He gathered his papers together at one side of his desk, addressed and sealed the letter, and was ready to go to bed. As he stood there, yawning and stretching, he was startled to hear the sound of running feet. Now he was sure it was a woman for he could hear her heels clicking on the uncarpeted back stairs.

Governor McKinney raced out into the hall and began running toward the stairway.

"Who is it? Who is it, I said. Stop! I know you are there." He threw open the door of the stairway as he called out but no one answered. When he reached the curve of the stairs where the light threw shadows on the wall and chased away some of the darkness, he was sure he would see someone but the stairway was empty. He did notice that the door at the top of the stairs was standing open a few inches. This was odd for the stairway was seldom used. But if he had heard someone, there was certainly no one there now.

The governor shook his head in bewilderment. Perhaps he had only imagined the sound was inside. It might have been the clatter of horses hoofs on the pavement somewhere out in the darkness. He decided he would go to his own room and go to bed. As he opened the door of his room he sprang back in amaze-

The governor of Virginia lives in a haunted mansion.

ment. A beautiful young woman was seated by the window wearing a long taffeta dress.

"I beg your pardon. I don't believe we have met," said the governor. The lady did not answer him or even turn her head. Governor McKinney backed hastily out the door and entered his wife's room across the hall.

"My dear, I wish you had told me you were using my bedroom as a guest room tonight," said the gover-

nor. Mrs. McKinney was amazed and puzzled. "We have no guests tonight. What do you mean?"

"I mean there is a strange woman sitting beside the window in my bedroom and she has no manners at all for she even refused to answer me when I spoke to her."

This was enough to get Mrs. McKinney out of bed and she and the governor crossed the hall and opened the door to his room. The lamp was lit, the chair drawn close to the table as if someone had been sitting there, but there was no lady in a long taffeta dress to be seen.

After that night the governor's brother heard the lady and chased her down the back stairs, a butler heard the footsteps and followed them into the basement and now, the present governor of Virginia, Linwood Holton, says he believes she may still be there. He has been awakened at night by the sound of ghostly footsteps and recently an entire row of paintings was found face downward.

"There was no wind, nothing to move them," says Holton, who finds it all very interesting.

But one governor was not at all happy about the ghost. He never stayed there alone at night if he could help it. Often he would call his friends and ask them to come and spend the night with him for he never knew

He never knew when he would hear the sound of the footsteps on the back stairs.

when he would hear the sound of the footsteps on the back stairs of the empty house.

All who have seen the ghost say she is young and beautiful. She only appears to a few people and does not allow everyone to see her. But through the years strange noises, voices, and footsteps have been reported in the Governor's Mansion. No one really knows who the lovely ghost is—or rather who she once was before she became a ghost—and no one really wants to hear or see her.

The Ghost Dog

THE GHOST THAT CHASES travelers down the old Buncombe Road has chosen a five-mile stretch of the road as his own. After dark is his time to roam, and he has frightened many people between the church cemetery and the big house at Goshen Hill near Newberry, South Carolina.

The big house that once belonged to Dr. George Douglass still stands but it is dark and empty now. It looks out over Buncombe Road, which was once the old stagecoach road. Traders used to drive along it with their covered wagons loaded with apples and chestnuts. Farmers rolled barrels of tobacco over it to Charleston, returning with salt, sugar, and tinware. Peo-

The big house that once belonged to Dr. George Douglass still stands.

ple did not always like to travel the road. It was dark and shadowy even during the daytime for the woods on either side were very thick.

One night in late October of 1855 a man who worked at the William Hardy farm became sick. Mr. Hardy told a boy named Jim Fairly who lived at his home to take a mule and ride four miles to get the doctor. It was after midnight when Dr. and Mrs. Douglass heard a clatter on their front porch and the sound of a boy screaming. The doctor ran down and opened the door. A trembling Jim stood in front of him crying, "Keep that thing from getting me." Dr. Douglass closed the door behind the boy and lit the lamp.

"Oh, Dr. Douglass, I am so scared I would have died if I hadn't gotten to your door when I did," said young Jim Fairly. "Mr. Hardy sent me to get you to come and see Sam because he's awful sick."

"Is Sam dying?" asked the doctor.

"No, Sam isn't dying. At least he wasn't when I left."

"Well, why are you so scared?" questioned Dr. Douglass.

"I was riding along and when I got to the church cemetery I heard a noise. I looked in back of me and saw the worst-looking creature I ever saw in my life. I hope I won't ever see such a sight again as long as I live."

"What foolish thing did you see?" asked the doctor,

who was still sleepy and not very happy at being waked up.

"It wasn't anything foolish. I was near the cemetery when I heard a noise. I looked around and saw the most terrible, biggest, whitest dog in the world. I stuck my heels in the mule and he broke out in such a fast run I was sure we were leaving that dog. All at once it got in front of the mule. He reared straight up in the air and I almost fell off. That dog was looking straight at us and my mule began shaking and running."

"How far did it follow you?"

"It stayed right in behind us and never left until I turned up the road to your house and started hollering."

The doctor went out into the yard and looked at the mule. The animal was dripping with sweat and still trembling. He called one of the men who worked for him and had him take the mule to the barn and give the frightened boy a place to sleep for the night.

Early that morning Dr. Douglass and the boy rode together to the Hardy house. All along the way Jim pointed out different places where "the dog came out last night." The doctor's own horse kept shying but he didn't see anything himself.

However another doctor who rode along the stage-coach route often saw the ghost dog. In fact his own dog would refuse to follow him along one stretch of the

The doctor ran down and opened the door.

"I looked around and saw the most terrible, biggest, whitest dog in the world."

road. When they reached this place, his dog would leave the road and cut through the woods. He would come back to his master only after Dr. Coefield had passed the trail of the white ghost dog. For more than a hundred years people who live near Newberry have been telling stories about the hound of Goshen.

Some say they have seen the huge white figure of the dog leap through a closed iron gate or lunge out of the bushes beside the road. Animals on the road often behave as if they are badly frightened and always seem to be the first to feel the presence of the ghost dog.

Joe Baldwin's Light

IT WAS A DARK and rainy night in 1867 as the train neared Wilmington, North Carolina. The wood-burning engine went chuga, chuga, chuga, chuga—spewing a shower of soot and sparks out of the smokestack and back upon the passenger coaches.

Conductor Joe Baldwin didn't worry much about that now for he was almost home. He looked at the hands of his big, round gold watch.

It was close to midnight. Opening the door at the foot of the coach, he stretched out his foot to step over to the next car. But his foot stopped in mid-air. There was no car ahead of him!

He was in the last coach and somehow it had come

uncoupled and broken loose from the rest of the train. When he saw what had happened, Baldwin was very frightened. He knew another train was following and he could feel his coach traveling slower and slower and finally coming to a stop. Joe Baldwin raced back to the rear of the coach carrying his lantern to signal the other train.

Wrenching open the heavy door, he was out on the platform with one leap. Less than a mile away, he saw a light coming out of the blackness. It was the single fiery eye of another train. He began to swing his lantern. As the light of the coming train burned more brightly behind him, Joe Baldwin swung his lantern ever more furiously.

But it was no use. The train was upon him. The engine hurtled into the rear of his runaway coach with a crunching crash and demolished it. In the collision Joe's head was severed from his body. His lantern arched high into the sky before it fell landing beside the tracks.

It was not long afterward that people who lived near Maco Station, where the accident had happened, began to talk of something very strange. They told of seeing a mysterious light moving down the tracks, particularly on dark and rainy nights. It would begin as a small flicker over the left rail. Then it would grow brighter

Joe Baldwin swung his lantern furiously but the train was
upon him.

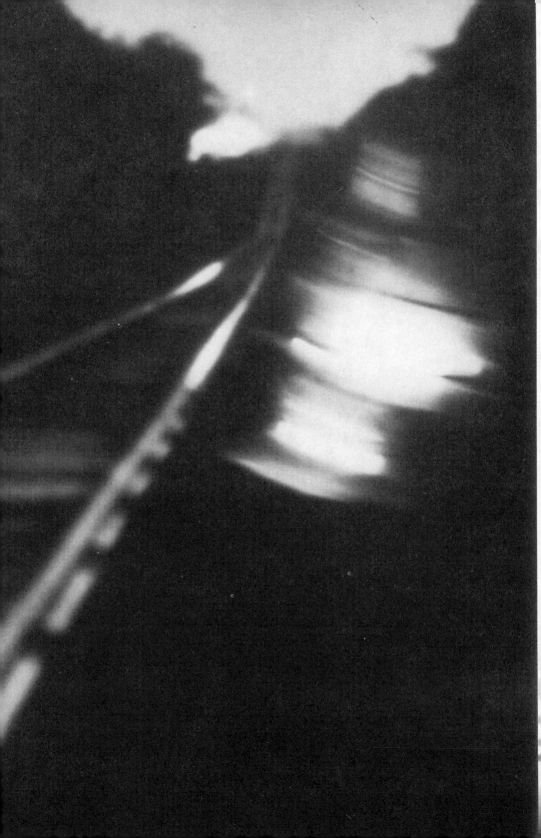

as it approached the station. Coming slowly up the track, it would swing from side to side just like a lantern.

People said that the ghost of Joe Baldwin had come back to look for his head. The light would finally stop and hang suspended in the air. Then, very slowly, it would go back down the track, becoming just a pinpoint of light before it disappeared into the distance. Many visitors began to come and watch it. When the light was first seen there were no roads anywhere about. And, of course, there were no electric lights or cars.

Railroad engineers often saw the light from their cab and thought it was a real signal light. Their brakes would screech as they brought their train to a stop. But no sooner did they stop than the light would disappear. Finally, the railroad ordered its signalmen at Maco to use two lanterns. And, they told the engineers not to stop if they saw just one light along the tracks there.

Scientists have come and investigated the light and soldiers have even roped off the area and tried to capture "Joe's light." But no one has ever been able to explain it.

They told of seeing a mysterious light moving down the tracks.